Our World
MOUNTAINS

Keith Lye

Silver Burdett Press
Morristown, New Jersey

Titles in this series

Mountains

Rivers and Lakes

Deserts

Jungles and Rainforests

Polar Regions

Seas and Oceans

First published in 1986 by
Wayland (Publishers) Ltd
61 Western Road, Hove
East Sussex BN3 1JD

Adapted and first published in
the United States in 1987 by
Silver Burdett Press,
250 James Street,
Morristown, New Jersey 07960

Designed by Malcolm Smythe.

U.S. edition edited by Joanne Fink

Library of Congress Cataloging-in-Publication Data

Lye, Keith.
    Mountains.

    (Our world)
    Includes bibliographies and index.
    Summary: Examines different kinds of mountains, their
wildlife, and their inhabitants and stresses the need for
conservation of mountain resources.
    1. Mountains—Juvenile literature. [1. Mountains]
I. Title. II. Series: Our world (Morristown, N. J.)
GB512.L94 1987   551.4'32   87-9850
ISBN 0-382-09498-0

Typeset by Alphabet Limited, London
Printed in Italy by G. Canale & C.S.p.A., Turin.

Front cover main picture Macchapuchhare, the "Fish
Tail" mountain in the Annapurna range of the Himalayas.

Front cover inset An alpine marmot.

Back cover Painacota Volcano and Chungará Lake, Chile.

Contents

The magic of mountains

The sight of distant, snow-capped mountains fills most people with awe and admiration for their dazzling beauty. The ancient Greeks believed that their greater gods dwelt upon Mount Olympus. Likewise the Nepalese, who live in the shadow of the world's highest peak, Mount Everest, used to think that mountaintops were the dwelling places of gods. In the western world, until about 200 years ago, people feared mountains. Travelers risked ambush by bandits, and were at the mercy of avalanches, landslides, and sudden weather changes, which made them lose their way. In the late eighteenth century, when the Swiss scientist Horace Bénédict de Saussure wanted to explore Mont Blanc, the highest peak in the Alps, local people told him that the way to the top was blocked by demons and dragons.

Today, modern methods of transportation (for example, jet airplanes and cablecars) have turned many mountain regions into year-round recreational areas. Their mystery has diminished, but they still attract people who love adventure, such as mountaineers, and those who simply enjoy the scenery and tranquillity.

Every continent has mountains. Some, such as the Himalayas, Alps, Rockies, and Andes, are "fold" mountains. There are also "dome" mountains and "block" mountains – all formed by different geological forces. Volcanoes, too, can be found on all the continents except Australia.

Mountains occur not only on land, but also beneath the oceans, which mask about 71 percent of the earth's surface. For example, enormous ridges 1.2 to 2.5 miles (2 to 4km) high and up to 2,500 miles (4,000km) wide rise from the ocean floor. Some ocean ridges are more than 24,900 miles (40,000km) long and, in places, they reach the surface to form such islands as Iceland and Ascension in the Atlantic Ocean. Volcanic mountains also rise from parts of the seabed and some of them form islands.

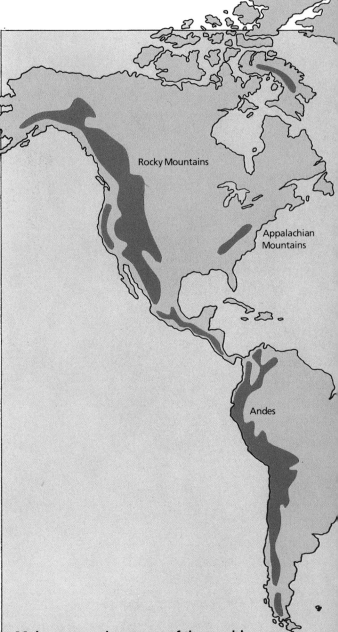

Major mountain ranges of the world
Mountains are found on every continent. The highest range in the world is the Himalayas. Other major ranges include the Rocky Mountains, the Andes, and the Alps. These high mountains are relatively young in the earth's history. Less spectacular, but much older, are the Appalachian Mountains, in the eastern United States.

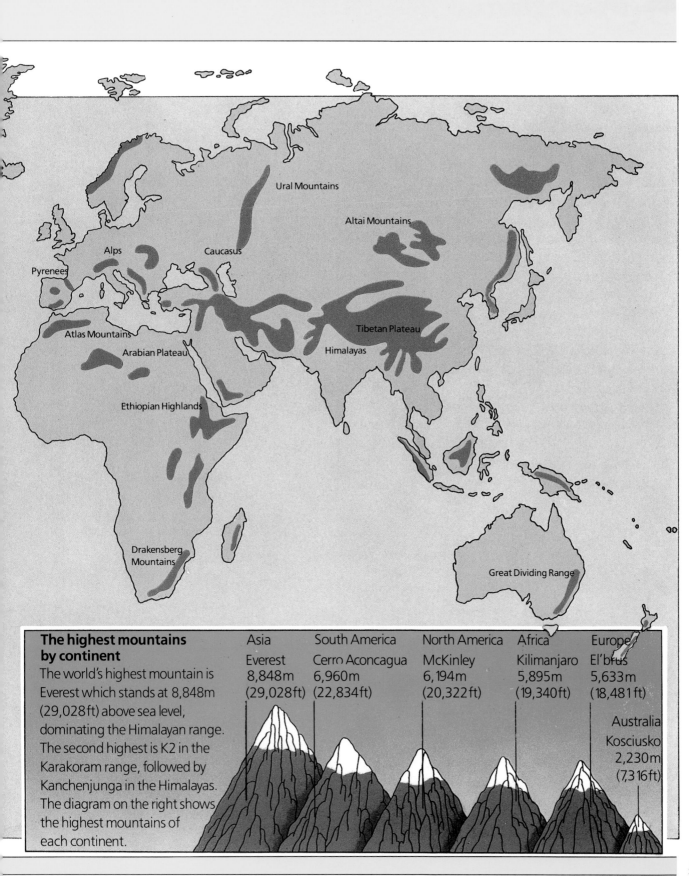

Ural Mountains

Altai Mountains

Alps

Caucasus

Pyrenees

Atlas Mountains

Arabian Plateau

Ethiopian Highlands

Tibetan Plateau

Himalayas

Drakensberg
Mountains

Great Dividing Range

The highest mountains by continent

The world's highest mountain is Everest which stands at 8,848m (29,028ft) above sea level, dominating the Himalayan range. The second highest is K2 in the Karakoram range, followed by Kanchenjunga in the Himalayas. The diagram on the right shows the highest mountains of each continent.

Asia	South America	North America	Africa	Europe
Everest	Cerro Aconcagua	McKinley	Kilimanjaro	El'brus
8,848m	6,960m	6,194m	5,895m	5,633m
(29,028ft)	(22,834ft)	(20,322ft)	(19,340ft)	(18,481ft)

Australia
Kosciusko
2,230m
(7,316ft)

The birth of a mountain

Fold mountains take millions of years to form. In fact, the Alps and Himalayas are probably still rising, although so slowly that scientists cannot be certain of it. However, between 1943 and 1951, scientists had a unique chance to study the formation of a volcanic mountain nearly 200 miles (320 km) west of Mexico City.

The story began in a field owned by a Mexican farmer. The field contained a small, strange hole that had been there for many years. On February 20, 1943, after as many as 300 earth tremors had rocked the area over the previous three weeks, the farmer noticed a fissure (crack) in the ground. The fissure passed through the mysterious hole, from which smoke appeared to be rising. The "smoke" was in fact fine dust and hot rocky ash, that had piled up around the hole.

Later that day, glowing lumps of rock were hurled from the hole, setting fire to trees. The alarmed people of the nearby village of San Juan Parangaricutiro sent representatives to see what was happening. They found that the hole was now much bigger, and glowing stones were exploding from it into the air. These are known as volcanic bombs.

The next day, the stones and ash had built up an infant mountain, which the Mexican government named the Volcáno de Parícutin. Over the next week, the explosions increased in frequency and, by February 27, the cone around the hole was about 490 ft (150 m) high. In March, huge clouds of ash exploded from the hole. Some of the ash fell on Mexico City.

In June 1943, streams of lava poured down the sides of the cone. Later on, more lava flowed from fissures around the cone. Soon San Juan Parangaricutiro was covered by lava, except for its church tower. Parícutin went on erupting until just after its ninth birthday in 1951, when the cone stood 1,350 ft (410 m) higher than the original field.

Left In 1963 a spectacular eruption marked the birth of Surtsey, a new volcanic island south of Iceland. The island was formed from magma rising to the surface from the deep Atlantic Ridge.

Right The church spire of San Juan Parangaricutiro rising above rocks of solidified lava, which flowed from the volcano Parícutin in June 1943.

Moving continents

Scientists have put forward many theories to explain how mountains are formed. One suggested that the earth was shrinking and that this made its surface wrinkle, like a dried-up apple. But research in the last forty years has revealed that powerful forces inside the earth are constantly changing the planet's surface by moving the continents around. It is these forces that are responsible for most mountain building.

The earth consists of a core, a mantle, and a thin crust. The core probably consists mostly of iron. The center of the core is solid, but around it is a molten outer core. Enclosing the core is the 1,800 mile (2,900 km) thick mantle. The mantle consists of dense (heavy) rocks, which are mostly solid. But there is a semi-molten layer, called the asthenosphere, near the top. "Floating" on the asthenosphere are the solid rocks in the top of the mantle and the overlying crust. These solid rocks are split into large sections, or "plates," which are from 43 to 62 miles (70 to 100 km) thick.

Recent studies have shown that there are currents in the semi-molten asthenosphere that move the plates around. The movements are slow, ranging from 0.4 to 4 inches (1 to 10 cm) a year. But over millions of years, these movements have totally changed the world map. Geologists now know that about 180 million years ago, there was only one huge continent, surrounded by one vast ocean. That old continent broke up and the parts drifted away from each other to form the modern continents. Between them were the newly formed oceans.

The edges of some plates can be seen on the surface. The San Andreas Fault in the western United States is a huge crack in the crust where two plates are moving alongside each other. But the oceans hide many plate edges from view. Plate edges run through the ocean ridges and also along ocean trenches, the deepest parts of the oceans.

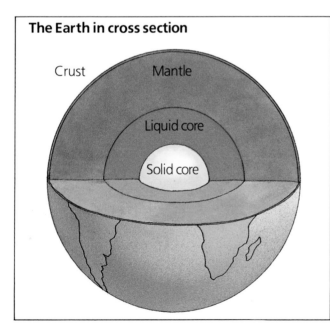

The Earth in cross section. On the surface are "floating" plates which move around as a result of currents within the semi-molten layers of the upper mantle.

As plates move, long cracks called faults open up. When blocks of land sink between faults, deep rift valleys are formed, like this one in Kenya.

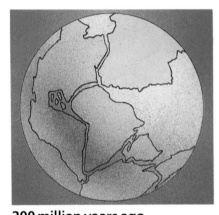

200 million years ago

One enormous super-continent was surrounded by a huge ocean. India was wedged between Africa and Australia at this time.

65 million years ago

As the plates slowly moved apart, new oceans were formed, separating the continents. Very gradually, the continents shifted position.

Today

The continents occupy their present, familiar positions. India has joined Eurasia and the Himalayas form the boundary.

The earth's crust is divided into plates that are slowly, but constantly moving. In 50 million years, Africa will join southern Europe, and the Mediterranean Sea will close up. Arabia will join Asia as the Red Sea widens. The boundary lines between plates are areas of intense geological activity — where plates collide or move apart, volcanoes and earthquakes occur, and mountains are formed.

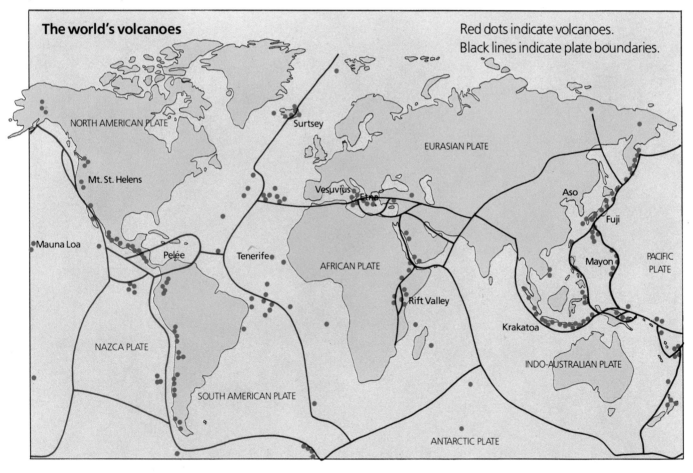

The world's volcanoes

Red dots indicate volcanoes.
Black lines indicate plate boundaries.

NORTH AMERICAN PLATE
Surtsey
EURASIAN PLATE
Mt. St. Helens
Vesuvius
Etna
Aso
Fuji
Mauna Loa
Pelée
Tenerife
AFRICAN PLATE
Mayon
PACIFIC PLATE
NAZCA PLATE
Rift Valley
Krakatoa
INDO-AUSTRALIAN PLATE
SOUTH AMERICAN PLATE
ANTARCTIC PLATE

Mountain building

Running through the centers of the ocean ridges are valleys, which are the boundaries between the plates on either side of them. Beneath the valleys, movements of molten rock in the asthenosphere are pulling the plates apart, as shown in the diagram on this page. As the plates move apart, hot molten rock, called magma, wells up from the asthenosphere to fill the gaps. When the magma cools and hardens, it forms new crustal rocks. This process is called "ocean spreading," because it is slowly widening the oceans. Sometimes, magma piles up to form underwater volcanoes, some of which eventually become islands. An example is Surtsey, which emerged off Iceland in 1963.

Along the ocean trenches, crustal rock is being destroyed. This is happening because two plates are pushing against each other, making the edge of one plate slip down beneath the other. Geologists call these places "subduction zones." As the plate descends into the hot mantle, it melts to form magma. Some of this magma rises up through the overlying plate and some reaches the surface through volcanoes.

When the downward movement of the plate finally ceases, the colliding plates still go on pushing against each other in what geologists call a

The diagram shows how the plates in the top part of the Earth move. Currents of molten rock are pulling plates apart along the ocean ridges, widening the oceans.

In places called subduction zones, one plate is being pushed beneath another. As it descends, it melts, forming magma for volcanoes which occur alongside the zone.

When two plates collide, the rocks between the plates are squeezed upward by enormous pressure into great folds. These folds become mountains. The Himalayas and the Alps are both examples of mountains formed in this way.

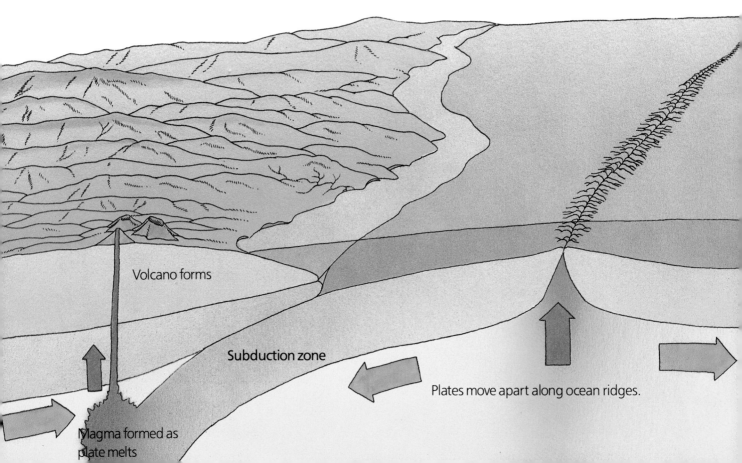

Volcano forms

Subduction zone

Plates move apart along ocean ridges.

Magma formed as plate melts

"collision zone." The sideways pressure squeezes the rocks on the seabed between the plates into loops, or folds, which rise upward to form fold mountain ranges, such as the Himalayas. This explains why fossils of sea creatures are found in rocks near the top of Mount Everest.

Plate movements are also responsible for block mountains. They are formed when the moving plates cause great tension in nearby rocks. This tension creates long fissures, or faults, in the rocks. Blocks of land that slip down between faults create steep-sided rift valleys. Other blocks are pushed upward to form block mountains.

Left The fold mountains of the Bernese Oberland in the Swiss Alps began to form 26 million years ago.

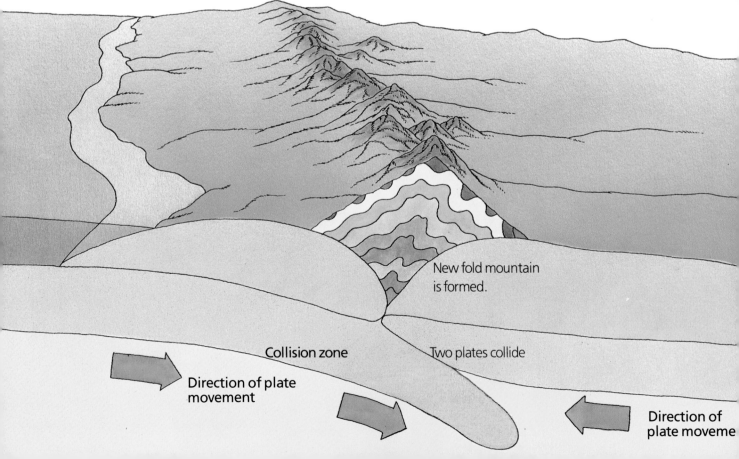

New fold mountain is formed.

Collision zone

Two plates collide

Direction of plate movement

Direction of plate moveme

Volcanoes

The ancient Romans thought that eruptions on the Italian island of Vulcano, from which the word volcano comes, were caused by the blacksmith god Vulcan. However, scientists now know that most volcanoes are caused by plate movements and lie near plate edges, namely along the ocean ridges and over the subduction zones. There are a few volcanoes, like those in Hawaii in the North Pacific Ocean, that are far from plate edges. Scientists think that they lie above "hot spots," or sources of radioactive heat, in the mantle.

The world has about 850 active volcanoes, many of which are concealed by the oceans. Active volcanoes are those that have erupted in recent times. An average of twenty to thirty volcanoes erupt every year. The other active volcanoes are dormant ("sleeping"). Erosion wears away extinct volcanoes and often only the hard neck, or pipe, remains. For example, Arthur's Seat, a hill in Edinburgh in central Scotland, is the remainder of a volcano that was active 325 million years ago.

Anak Krakatoa, Indonesia, is a classic explosive volcano. It explodes, emitting a towering cloud of ash and dust.

Explosive volcano

Intermediate volcano

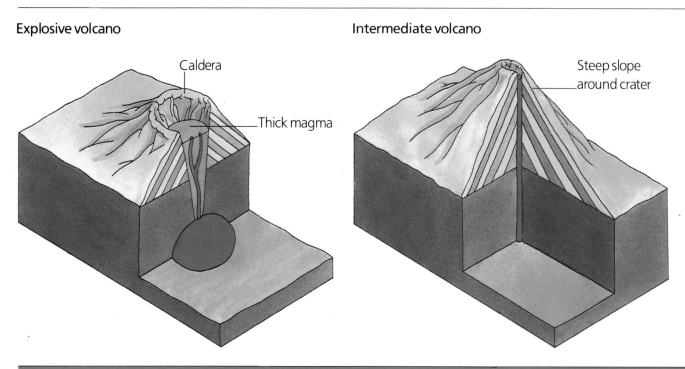

Caldera

Thick magma

Steep slope around crater

Volcanoes are divided into three main types: explosive, quiet, and intermediate. Volcanic explosions occur when gases and steam trapped in thick, pasty magma expand. Eventually, they shatter the magma into fragments ranging from dust and ash to loaf-sized lumps, called volcanic bombs. These fragments are hurled into the air during eruptions. By contrast, quiet volcanoes contain runny magma, which does not explode. Instead it flows from the volcanoes in long streams of red-hot lava.

Most volcanoes erupt sometimes explosively and sometimes quietly. Such intermediate volcanoes contain alternating layers of ash and hardened lava flows.

Volcanoes often cause great destruction, but they have also had a constructive role throughout the earth's history. Eruptions release gases and water vapor from rocks, and so they have helped to create the atmosphere and the oceans. Volcanic soils are among the world's most fertile.

Kilauea Iki, Hawaii, is a quiet volcano. Fountains of runny lava caused by small explosions are spectacular sights.

Volcanoes erupt in two main ways. One is known as an explosive eruption. The magma is thick and pasty and contains a lot of explosive gases. Eruptions are marked by huge explosions, sometimes destroying part of the volcano itself. The magma is shattered into lumps of cinder and ash. Cinder cones are steep-sided (far left). In other types of eruptions, liquid lava flows from the volcano, and there are no big explosions. However, huge fountains of glowing, runny lava often appear. These are called quiet eruptions. Such volcanic mountains are gently sloping (right). Most volcanoes, however, are intermediate. Sometimes they erupt explosively, and sometimes quietly. They are composed of alternate layers of ash and lava. The lower slopes of this type of volcano are gentle, but become steep near the top (left).

Quiet volcano

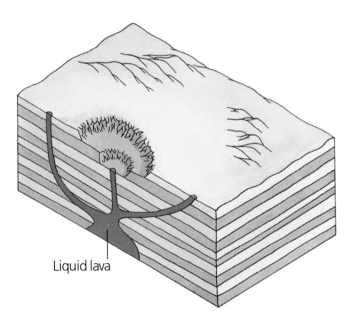

Liquid lava

Fold mountains

Fold mountains are formed when two plates push against each other. The enormous pressure squeezes level layers of rock between the plates into huge folds.

Simple folding created the Jura Mountains along France's border with Switzerland. If the folds in the Jura Mountains were stretched out flat, the width of the mountain range would be increased by only about 3 miles (5km). In the Himalayas, the rocks have been compressed by as much as 404 miles (650km). Here the folds are extremely complicated. They include recumbent (overturned) folds and nappes – folds that have broken away and have been pushed forward over other rocks.

The Himalayas were created by a plate collision that began fifty to sixty million years ago. One plate supported the Indian subcontinent. This plate had originally been wedged between Africa and Australia in the ancient supercontinent of 180 million years ago. When the Indian plate broke away, it drifted toward the Eurasian plate. Between the two lay an ancient ocean – the Tethys Sea. As the plates pressed against each other, the rock beds on the floor of the Tethys Sea were bent upward to form the Himalayas. The Tethys Sea disappeared when India was joined to Asia.

Other fold mountain ranges were formed in similar ways. The Alps, the youngest of the world's

Alongside the Yerupaja glacier, Peru, are clear rock folds.

Right The majestic Himalayas were formed when India collided with Asia.

great ranges, began to rise about twenty-six million years ago, when the African plate pushed smaller plates against the Eurasian plate.

Mountain building continues all the time. For example, ocean spreading is slowly widening the Red Sea between northeastern Africa and Arabia. This is pushing Arabia northeastward. In about 50 million years, the Persian Gulf will have closed up, and a new fold mountain range will exist.

Lateral pressure squeezes rock layers into folds. Downfolds are called synclines, and upfolds anticlines.

Some folds tilt over at an angle. Such overturned folds are called recumbent folds.

Sometimes the upper part of a fold breaks away and is pushed forward. Such sheared folds are called nappes.

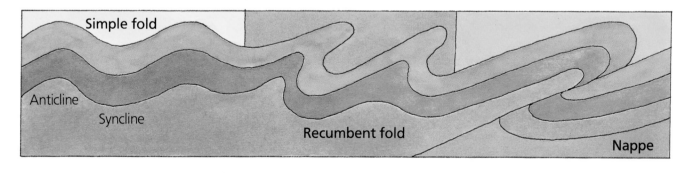

Simple fold

Anticline

Syncline

Recumbent fold

Nappe

Dome and block mountains

Besides fold mountains and volcanoes, there are two other main types of mountains: dome mountains and block mountains.

Dome mountains are formed when molten magma rises from the mantle, but instead of reaching the surface through volcanoes, it lifts up the overlying rocks to form a dome. The magma then cools and hardens to form granite. Later, when the overlying rocks are worn away, the granite appears on the surface. The Black Hills of South Dakota are an example of dome mountains. So, on a much smaller scale, is the British Lake District.

Block mountains form when moving plates stretch and crack rocks, forming faults in the earth's crust. Rocks slide up and down these faults. When a block of land slips down between faults, a rift valley, or graben, is formed. The land on either side of the steep-walled rift valley forms block mountains. For example, the Vosges in north-eastern France and the Black Forest in Germany are block mountains bordering a rift valley containing the Rhine River. The Red Sea occupies a similar, larger rift valley, bordered by block mountains in northeastern Africa and Arabia.

The Sierra Nevada in eastern California are block mountains. They are tilted blocks, whose eastern side has been uplifted. To the east of the Sierra Nevada is the Basin and Range region. The lower ranges in this area are all similar, uptilted blocks. The Great Dividing Range in eastern Australia was also formed mostly by uplift, although the rocks are the remains of an extremely ancient mountain range.

Some mountains occur along the edges of high plateaus (tablelands), which have also been uplifted. The Drakensberg range on South Africa's border with Lesotho is the uptilted edge of a huge plateau that forms most of southern Africa.

Molten magma rises under pressure through the rocks in the Earth's crust. Rising bodies of magma can arch up overlying rocks into dome mountains. The magma then cools to form rocks like granite. Rocks often move along huge fractures, called faults, causing earthquakes. Blocks of land that are pushed up between faults form block mountains. Blocks that slip down form steep rift valleys.

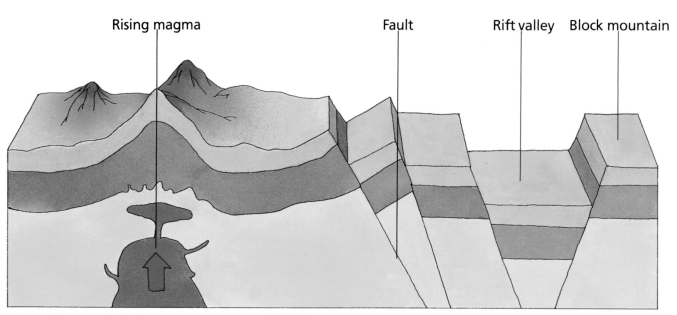

Rising magma   Fault   Rift valley   Block mountain

The Black Hills of South Dakota are a classic example of dome mountains.

El Capitan, a dramatic ice-worn cliff in the Sierra Nevada range in California.

Erosion

The surface of the earth is changing all the time. Even as mountains are rising upward, natural processes wear them down. These processes are called the forces of erosion. For example, frost action cracks and splits rocks in cold, wet mountain regions. This occurs because the ice that forms from water in rock crevices occupies over nine percent more space than the original water. The ice, therefore, exerts pressure on the sides of the cracks until the rocks split apart.

Rainwater also dissolves some rocks, such as limestone. And in hot deserts, the great temperature change from day to night causes rocks to crack and their surfaces to peel slowly away like the layers of an onion.

Broken fragments of rock tumble downhill and often pile up in heaps, called talus or scree. These fragments are eventually carried away by other natural forces, such as moving ice and rivers or streams.

Glaciers are long, moving tongues of ice that slide down mountain valleys. Their surfaces are often littered with shattered rocks. Other rocks are frozen into the bottoms and sides of the glaciers. They give the moving ice a cutting edge because they scrape away at the ground and wear away more rocks. Erosion by glaciers produces many characteristic features, including deep, U-shaped valleys, armchair-shaped basins called cirques, and sharp peaks called horns.

Fast-flowing mountain streams, swollen by heavy rain or melting snow, become raging torrents. They sweep pebbles and even boulders downhill. These loose rocks grind away at the beds of the streams, deepening them to form V-shaped valleys.

In deserts, floods caused by rare thunderstorms also erode mountains. But more important is wind erosion. Windblown sand acts much like the sandblasters used to clean dirty city buildings. It carves out caves and undercuts boulders.

Erosion by frost
Frost action occurs when water fills cracks in the rocks and freezes into ice. The ice takes up more space than water and so exerts pressure on the rock, widening the crack until the boulder splits. Shown at left is frost shattered debris alongside a cirque in the mountains of Wales, in Britain.

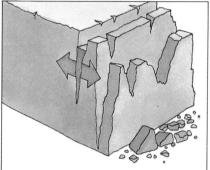

Erosion by glaciation

Glaciers transport shattered rocks downhill. These rocks scrape against the ground, wearing away the land to form deep U-shaped valleys. Shown at left is the classic U-shaped valley of Lauterbrunnen in Switzerland which was once occupied by a glacier.

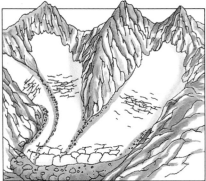

Erosion by wind and sand

Mountains in desert regions are eroded by wind and sand. The wind-blown sand eats away at rocks along lines of weakness, carving them into strange shapes. The picture shows the effect of wind erosion on the mountains of the Makran coast in southern Iran.

Landslides and volcanic eruptions

Erosion is usually a slow process. However, major changes to the landscape can occur in a matter of minutes.

On steep slopes, gravity pulls loose material downhill. For example, when soil grains absorb rainwater, the weight of the soil is increased and the soil moves downward. This is called soil creep. Sometimes soil creep occurs on a large scale, forming landslides. For example, heavy rains on a mountain slope in northern Italy in 1963 sent masses of soil and rock crashing into a reservoir. The reservoir overflowed, and floods destroyed a town below the dam. The world's worst landslide occurred in China in 1920, killing an estimated 180,000 people.

Avalanches happen when masses of snow slide downhill. Some start when snowbanks become top-heavy. Others are caused by earthquakes, thaws, and even sounds, such as rifle shots, that cause vibrations. Avalanches often carry soil, rock, and trees as they slide downhill.

Earthflows are movements of fine material, such as clay. Some earthflows occur when loose ash from volcanoes mixes with water. In 1985, an earthflow following an eruption of the volcano Nevado de Ruiz in Colombia killed as many as 25,000 people. Some volcanoes emit hot clouds of ash and gas. These clouds are called nuées ardentes. They race down the mountainsides and destroy everything in their path. In 1902, Mount Pelée on the island of Martinique erupted and a nuée ardente killed 30,000 people in the town of St. Pierre.

Observation stations are now positioned on many volcanoes. Specialists (sometimes known as volcanologists) study the behavior of the volcanoes, noting any changes in pressure, temperature, the composition of gases inside the volcano, earth tremors, and swellings in the ground. If they think an eruption is likely, they warn the local people to leave the area.

Left A volcanologist, wearing a heat resistant suit, measures the gas speed and temperature on Mount Etna.

Above right Following an earthquake in Peru in 1970, a huge mudflow swept through this valley.

Right An avalanche on the slope of Hium Chuli, in the Himalayas.

21

Heat and cold; wind and water

The weather and climate of mountains vary with height. The higher one goes, the thinner is the air and the lower the air pressure. On high slopes there is less air than at sea level to hold the heat that is reflected from the land. As a result, temperatures fall, on average, by 1.8°F (1°C) for every 490 feet (150m) gained in height.

Because temperatures decrease with height, high mountains, even on the equator, are always capped by snow and ice. The level above which snow remains throughout the year is called the snowline. Near the poles, the snowline is at sea level. In the Alps, it is about 9,000 feet (2,750m) above sea level, while, around the equator, it is between 17,060 and 17,980 feet (5,200–5,480m) high.

Mountains are among the windiest and wettest places. The world's highest recorded wind speed 231mph (371kph) was recorded on the exposed upper slopes of Mount Washington, in the White Mountains of New Hampshire.

Orographic rainfall is the main type of rain in mountains. It occurs when warm, moist winds from the sea blow upward along mountain slopes. As the winds rise, the air is cooled. Because cold air cannot hold as much water vapor as warm air, cooling makes invisible water vapor condense (liquefy) into tiny, but visible water droplets or ice crystals. Billions of these droplets or crystals form clouds. Gradually, the droplets and crystals collide and grow in size until they become heavy enough to fall as raindrops or snowflakes.

Winds often lose most of their moisture on the windward slopes of mountains. But when the winds descend the leeward slopes, they become warmer and evaporate moisture from the land. These dry leeward slopes are said to form a "rain shadow" area.

Right At over 22,000ft (7,000m), these peaks of the Peruvian Andes are permanently snow-capped. The snow melts on the lower slopes, allowing vegetation to flourish.

A diagram of orographic rainfall. As the moist winds from the sea rise higher up the mountainside, and the air temperature becomes cooler, the water vapor condenses into clouds, finally falling as rain or snow. The right-hand side of the diagram shows the leeward side of the mountain, which forms a rain shadow area.

Moist winds condense into rain clouds

Rain shadow area

Plants

Because mountains are colder at the summit and warmer toward the base, each vegetation type prefers a certain part of the mountain. So high mountains can be divided into vegetation zones.

Below the snowline is a treeless alpine (or tundra) zone, which resembles the tundra regions in the Arctic. The plants here must survive intense cold and include mosses, lichens, short grasses, sedges and low, flowering plants. The summer growing season is short, and so most alpine plants are perennials, which take several years to flower and set seed. Typical alpine plants are just an inch or so tall, and form dense cushions or rosette shapes. To survive the strong winds, most plants are virtually stemless and have long roots, which act as anchors. Many plants are covered by hairs that let in heat and light, but reduce air movement. To keep warm, some plants contain rich cell fluids that act like antifreeze – the alpine soldanella produces heat sufficient to melt snow.

Alpine plants are specially adapted to survive at high altitudes despite their seemingly fragile appearance. Although they thrive at the lowest temperatures and on gravelly soil or bare rock, alpine flowers are highly colorful to attract insects to pollinate them. Shown above is the spring gentian (*Gentiana verna*) and below the moss campion (*Silene acaulis*).

Lower down, the alpine zone merges into a shrub zone with dwarf trees. This zone ends at the treeline, or timberline – the upper limit of tree growth. Its height varies according to the temperature, rainfall, exposure to sunlight, and the latitude. In much of Scandinavia, the treeline is below 1,970 feet (600m). Around the equator it is above 13,120 feet (4,000m).

In the northern hemisphere, the highest forests consist of coniferous trees, such as fir, pine, and spruce. With their thick bark and needle-like leaves, which reduce water loss, these evergreens can survive long, cold winters.

Below the coniferous forests are mixed forests of conifers and deciduous trees, such as beech, chestnut, and oak, which shed their leaves in winter. Lower still are deciduous forests.

In tropical regions, that are too hot for conifers, the slopes are covered by dense, evergreen "cloud" forests, which merge into true tropical rainforest or savanna (tropical grassland).

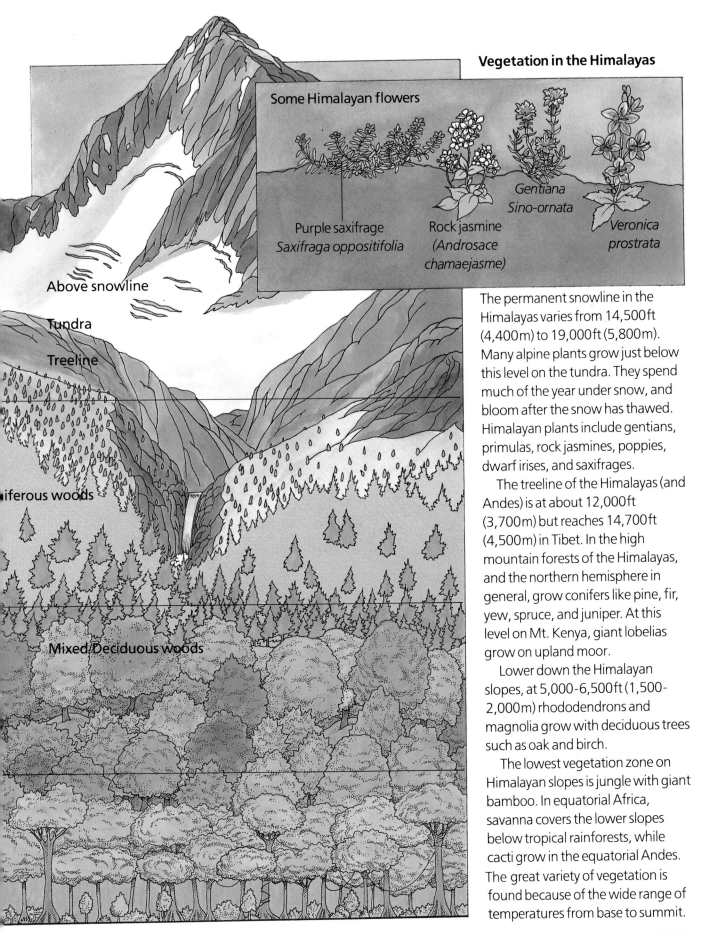

Vegetation in the Himalayas

Some Himalayan flowers

Purple saxifrage
Saxifraga oppositifolia

Rock jasmine
(Androsace chamaejasme)

Gentiana Sino-ornata

Veronica prostrata

Above snowline

Tundra

Treeline

...iferous woods

Mixed Deciduous woods

The permanent snowline in the Himalayas varies from 14,500ft (4,400m) to 19,000ft (5,800m). Many alpine plants grow just below this level on the tundra. They spend much of the year under snow, and bloom after the snow has thawed. Himalayan plants include gentians, primulas, rock jasmines, poppies, dwarf irises, and saxifrages.

The treeline of the Himalayas (and Andes) is at about 12,000ft (3,700m) but reaches 14,700ft (4,500m) in Tibet. In the high mountain forests of the Himalayas, and the northern hemisphere in general, grow conifers like pine, fir, yew, spruce, and juniper. At this level on Mt. Kenya, giant lobelias grow on upland moor.

Lower down the Himalayan slopes, at 5,000-6,500ft (1,500-2,000m) rhododendrons and magnolia grow with deciduous trees such as oak and birch.

The lowest vegetation zone on Himalayan slopes is jungle with giant bamboo. In equatorial Africa, savanna covers the lower slopes below tropical rainforests, while cacti grow in the equatorial Andes. The great variety of vegetation is found because of the wide range of temperatures from base to summit.

25

Animals

Like plants, mountain animals show certain adaptations to their environment. Many animals have larger hearts and lungs and more red blood cells than similar animals in lowland regions. Thick coats offer protection against the cold, while the soft pads on the hooves of some animals act like rubber suction cups to grip rocky surfaces.

Among the large mammals in the alpine zone are wild sheep, such as bighorns, and various wild goats, including the agile Eurasian ibex and chamois, and the Asian markhor. These animals live on the high alpine pastures in summer, but seek shelter in the valleys in winter. The only member of the cattle family fully adapted to mountains is the yak, which lives in the Tibetan plateaus to an altitude of 20,000 feet (6,000m). Its shaggy coat enables it to survive temperatures of $-104°F$ ($-40°C$). In the lower forests bears may be found.

Small mammals include snow hares, stoats, and marmots, that build up layers of fat in summer and hibernate in winter. Others, such as pikas, spend much of the summer piling up food stores for the winter. Few pure carnivores live in high mountain zones, but pumas, snow leopards, and wolves inhabit the alpine zone in summer.

Flying creatures have to survive windy conditions. Insects above the treeline are wingless or have small wings which they seldom use. Butterflies generally only visit lower mountain pastures, but the beautiful Apollo butterfly reaches 18,000 feet (5,500m) in the Himalayas. Some large birds of prey such as golden eagles, buzzards, and falcons are strong enough to contend with fierce winds. Scavenging condors and lammergeiers (bearded vultures) also soar at great heights. Other birds, such as Alpine choughs, wall-creepers, and sparrow-like accentors stay close to the ground when strong winds blow.

The alpine hare (*Lepus timidus*) can adapt its coloring to suit its mountain environment. As winter approaches, the hare's brown summer coat changes to white, providing excellent camouflage in the snow, and thus protecting the hare from its predators. The animal shown here has almost completed its winter moult.

Yak

Black bear and cub

Red panda

Animals of the Himalayas

Illustrated below are some typical animals of the Himalayan region. In the lower, tropical forests a variety of monkeys and birds are found, including fire-tailed sunbirds and grandalas. Black and brown bears live in higher forests, as do red pandas. Yaks, goats, and wild sheep are well adapted to the high, rocky areas, while small rodents like hares, marmots, voles, and pikas survive at 16,000ft (4,800m). Along with the very rare tiger, the beautiful snow leopard (pictured right) is sometimes seen. This animal ranges up to 18,000ft (5,500m) in summer.

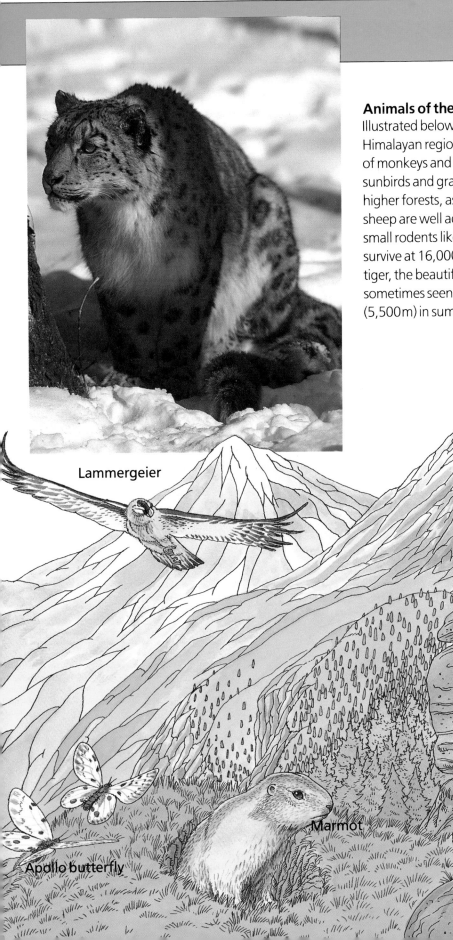

Lammergeier

Himalayan goat

Pika

Marmot

Apollo butterfly

People and mountains

Because the climate is often harsh, most mountain regions are sparsely populated. One hazard for visitors from lowlands is mountain sickness, or soroche. This is caused by the fact that the air is rarefied (thinner) and contains less oxygen than air near sea level. Symptoms include headaches, shortness of breath, and fast heartbeats. Some people suffer mountain sickness at a little less than 10,000 feet (3,000 m) above sea level, while others feel little effect until they reach heights of over 13,000 feet (4,000 m).

Unlike visitors used to lowlands, people such as the Sherpas of Nepal and the Amerindians of Peru, who live constantly at high levels, are not affected by mountain sickness. This is because they have bigger lungs that take in more air, more blood cells to carry the oxygen, and larger hearts to pump the blood cells swiftly around their bodies.

Most mountain people live in sheltered valleys or on level plateaus between ranges, and spend only part of the year on high mountain slopes. However, in tropical regions many people prefer to spend the summer in mountain resorts, because the plains become so hot. In hot deserts, including the Sahara, mountains often have more rainfall than the plains and so they provide pasture for animals belonging to nomads.

Because of the problems of living at high levels, most ancient civilizations developed on plains rather than on mountains. The most spectacular exception to this rule was the Inca civilization in the South American Andes Mountains. The Inca capital, Cuzco, stood at 11,450 feet (3,490 m). This great empire was conquered and destroyed by Spanish soldiers in the 1530s.

Until about 150 years ago, mountain ranges were regarded as obstacles to travel. But long railroad tunnels through mountains, and breathtaking, zigzag roads over high mountain passes have opened up mountains to tourists.

This Swiss railroad provides access to Schynige Platte at an altitude of 6,000 ft (2,000 m).

Right These people are returning to their summer mountain homes over the Rhotang Pass, India.

Below The ancient Inca settlement, Macchu Picchu, in the Peruvian Andes.

Farming in mountains

Farmers in Bolivia with their herds of llamas.

Rice and bananas grow successfully on these Indonesian terraces.

Many mountain people live by farming. Crops include cereals and fruit in temperate lands, and coffee and bananas in the tropics. Most crops are grown on valley floors or on the sunny lower slopes. In countries where farmland is scarce, such as Japan, Nepal, and the Philippines, farmers have built step-like terraces down mountain slopes. The terraces form level fields, often bounded by stone walls. They halt the rapid downflow of rainwater and thus keep it from washing away the soil.

Livestock rearing is important. Animals such as llamas in the Andes and yaks in the Himalayas are valuable sources of meat, milk, and hair used to make clothes. In many areas, including the European Alps, Scandinavia, and the North American Rocky Mountains, the rearing of dairy cattle and sheep are the chief farming activities. In these regions, the animals are kept in the valleys during winter, where they are housed in barns. In summer they are driven up to the alpine pastures to graze. The farmers also move to their high summer homes to make dairy products, including butter and cheese, and to harvest hay for the winter. This annual movement of farmers and animals in mountain regions is called transhumance. But like so many ancient practices, it is now becoming less common.

In winter, some farmers work as lumberjacks, for forestry is another important industry. The Rocky Mountain states contain softwoods, such as aspen, pine, and spruce, while the Appalachian Mountains have hardwood forests. Tropical mountain forests contain many valuable hardwoods, including ebony, mahogany, rosewood, and teak. Many countries have laws to control the cutting of trees for timber in mountains. If slopes are laid bare, the soil is exposed to the forces of erosion. This leaves a poor soil of little value to farmers and foresters.

Right The sheltered valley floor of Pokhara, Nepal, is used to grow bananas and to provide hay for livestock.

Mountain peoples

Most mountain dwellers are sturdy, tough, and independent people. For example, the Sherpas, who have become world famous as mountaineers, used to follow the trade routes between the lower parts of Nepal and neighboring Tibet, the so-called "roof of the world." They carried heavy loads of salt and wool from Tibet through passes reaching 18,045 feet (5,500m) above sea level, and returned with bags of cereals and other items produced in Nepal. The Nepalese Gurung people are also distinguished soldiers.

Another people, the Kurds, live in a mountainous region that includes parts of Turkey, the Soviet Union, Syria, Iraq, and Iran. Many Kurds would like to found their own nation, though so far their guerrilla forces have been defeated. Other famed guerrilla fighters include the Pathans, who live in the mountains of Afghanistan and Pakistan. Some Pathans are nomads, using camels as pack animals when driving their livestock to summer pastures.

Nomadism and transhumance are dominant features of Berber communities in the Atlas Mountains of Morocco and the Bakhtiari people of Iran. The Bakhtiari spend the winter in the foothills west of the rugged Zagros Mountains. In spring, when the winter pastures dry up, the Bakhtiari move eastward, climbing high passes and steep cliffs, and fording icy torrents to reach their summer pasture. Despite the chance to live in settled towns, most Bakhtiari still prefer their hard and often dangerous life.

In Europe, the Swiss people of the Alps and the Basques and Catalans of the Pyrenees (Spain) are other patriotic people who want to preserve their ancient traditions. In New Guinea, mainly in the west, there are small mountain communities who have had no contact with the outside world. They still lead a Stone Age way of life.

Some mountain peoples of the world

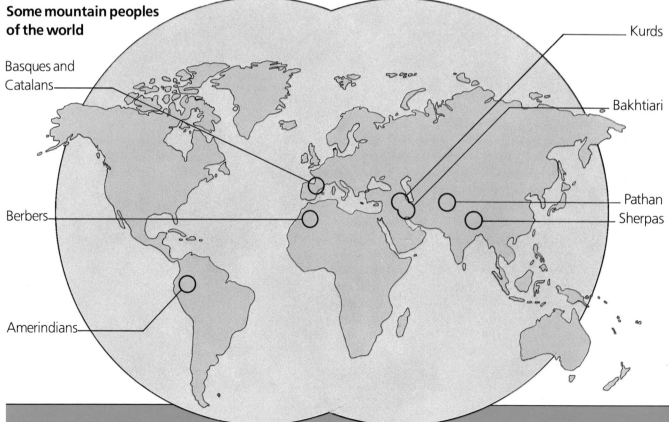

Basques and Catalans

Kurds

Bakhtiari

Berbers

Pathan

Sherpas

Amerindians

Above Some Amerindians washing their colorful clothes in a stream, which runs through Ecuador in the Andes.

Right Sherpas are well equipped for life at high altitudes. They carry cooking utensils and gather wood, so they can prepare hot food over a wood fire.

Left A map showing the distribution of some of the world's remote mountain peoples.

Hydroelectricity

In addition to forests and land for agricultural use, many mountain regions provide another vital natural resource – water. In sparsely populated mountain areas, dams are often constructed across rivers to create a store of water called a reservoir. The water stored in the reservoirs is then piped to more densely populated areas.

The water in reservoirs is also often used to produce hydroelectricity, or water power. The ancient Romans used water power to make flour.

They did this by connecting water wheels, turned by running water, to grinding stones. Since the 1880s, water power has been used to produce electricity.

Most hydroelectric power stations are situated at the dams that contain reservoirs. The water in the reservoir is used to turn the blades of motors, called turbines. The turbines then drive generators that produce electricity. Dams and hydroelectric power stations are costly to build, but once

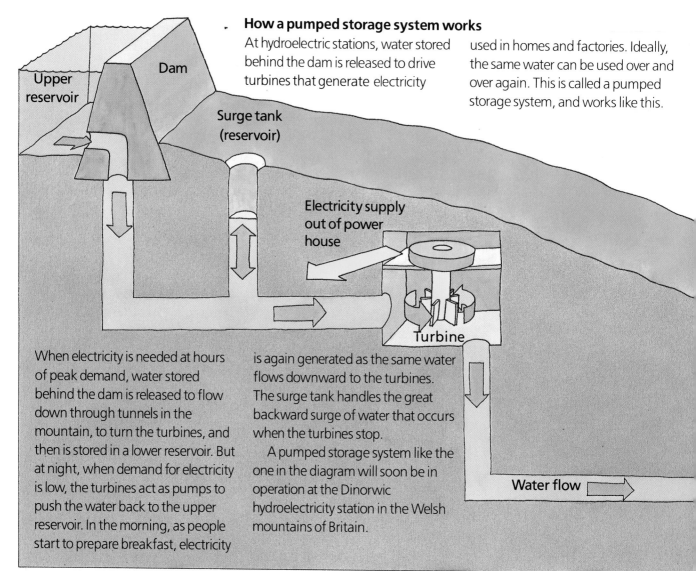

How a pumped storage system works

At hydroelectric stations, water stored behind the dam is released to drive turbines that generate electricity used in homes and factories. Ideally, the same water can be used over and over again. This is called a pumped storage system, and works like this.

When electricity is needed at hours of peak demand, water stored behind the dam is released to flow down through tunnels in the mountain, to turn the turbines, and then is stored in a lower reservoir. But at night, when demand for electricity is low, the turbines act as pumps to push the water back to the upper reservoir. In the morning, as people start to prepare breakfast, electricity is again generated as the same water flows downward to the turbines. The surge tank handles the great backward surge of water that occurs when the turbines stop.

A pumped storage system like the one in the diagram will soon be in operation at the Dinorwic hydroelectricity station in the Welsh mountains of Britain.

Millions of tons of water are retained by this vast concrete dam in the Swiss Alps.

complete, the production of hydroelectricity is cheap. It is also clean because no fuels are used. At some hydroelectric stations, part of the electricity output is used to pump water back to the high reservoir when the demand is low, as at night. This maintains a high water level in the reservoir.

Hydroelectricity is especially important in mountainous countries with plenty of water. For example, 70 percent of the electricity used in Switzerland and Colombia is generated at hydroelectric power stations.

Sometimes dams and reservoirs are interconnected in huge systems to generate vast amounts of electricity and to provide water for irrigation and other purposes. One of the largest of these systems is the Snowy Mountains Scheme in southeastern Australia. Completed in the 1970s, it contains 16 large dams, 9 power stations and 100 miles (160km) of tunnels to divert river water. Major projects also exist in the Soviet Union.

Right A hydroelectric power station in Roxburgh, New Zealand.

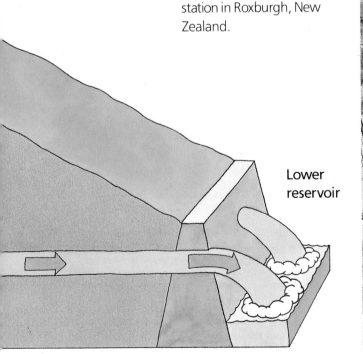

Lower reservoir

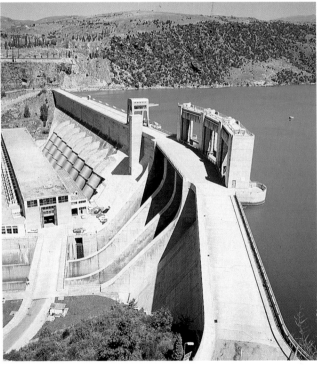

Minerals and mountains

When mountains are formed, hot magma often wells up beneath them. As it cools, the common minerals feldspar, quartz, and mica are the first to harden. Crystals of these minerals form granites. Other molten material, containing less common minerals, takes longer to cool. Sometimes this molten material is forced into cavities and cracks to form veins. These veins, therefore, often contain useful or rare minerals.

Traces of metals sometimes occur in stream beds. They originated in veins in rock carried by streams from distant mountains. The rock was gradually worn away. The discovery of rich gold veins led to many historic gold rushes in countries such as Australia, Canada, and the United States. During the Klondike Gold Rush in Canada's Yukon Territory in 1897-8, hundreds of miners risked their lives traveling across the mountains, but only a few were lucky. The mountains of the western United States contain many ghost towns, although some, including Aspen, a former silver mining center in Colorado, are now resorts.

The Andes Mountains are also rich in minerals. However, work in mines at high altitudes, as in Bolivia's tin mines, is hard because of the rarefied (thin) atmosphere.

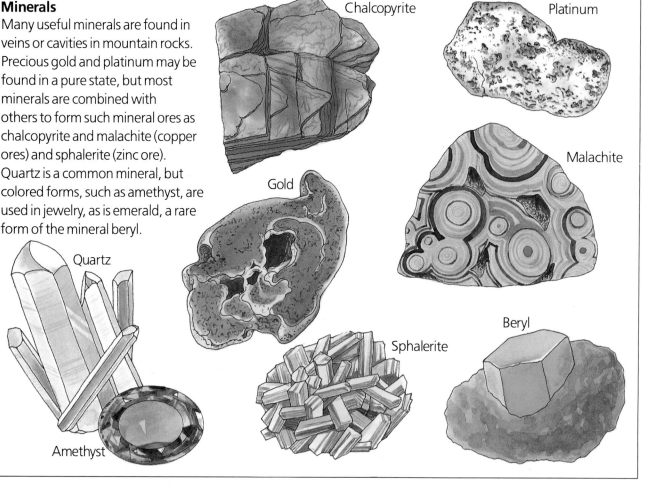

Minerals

Many useful minerals are found in veins or cavities in mountain rocks. Precious gold and platinum may be found in a pure state, but most minerals are combined with others to form such mineral ores as chalcopyrite and malachite (copper ores) and sphalerite (zinc ore). Quartz is a common mineral, but colored forms, such as amethyst, are used in jewelry, as is emerald, a rare form of the mineral beryl.

Chalcopyrite

Platinum

Malachite

Gold

Quartz

Beryl

Sphalerite

Amethyst

Tin slag heaps at a mine in the Bolivian Andes.

Mountains also yield building stone. Italy's Apennine Mountains contain many limestone and marble quarries. The famous Carrara quarry has provided top-quality marble for many sculptors, including Michelangelo (1475-1564).

Many minerals lie on or close to the surface. For example, some mountains in western Australia consist almost entirely of iron ore, and they are now being dug away. But open-cast mining is a threat to the beauty of mountains. Similarly, unsightly dumps of waste rock brought up from underground mines spoil the natural scenery of mountain regions.

Budie, a gold mining ghost town in California.

Mountaineering

Another aspect of mountains is their magnificent scenery and the challenge they present to rock climbers. Mountaineering has been a popular sport for about 200 years. The father of European mountaineering was the Swiss scientist Horace Bénédict de Saussure who, in 1787, climbed Mont Blanc, France, the highest peak in the Alps. His experiences inspired others and, between 1854 and 1865, the "golden age" of European mountaineering, most Alpine peaks were scaled.

In the nineteenth century mountaineers satisfied their love of adventure by traveling to other ranges. The climbers who stayed in Europe looked for more difficult routes to the tops of mountains already climbed. This led to rock climbing, the scaling of sheer rock faces.

In the early days, mountaineers used simple equipment, including *alpenstocks* – long, pointed walking sticks – and ladders. They wore spiked boots or *crampons* (metal frames with steel spikes,

which they strapped to their boots). The climbers used axes to cut steps in ice, and ropes to link the members of a climbing party together. For rock climbing, the most useful extra item was the *piton*, a metal spike hammered into rocks to give climbers a hold.

With new equipment and supplies of oxygen, mountaineers could tackle the world's highest peaks. European climbers went to the Himalayas in the 1880s, but no one could approach Mount Everest until 1921, when the Tibetan government first let foreign expeditions pass through its territory.

The greatest feats took place after 1947, when climbers were first allowed to enter Nepal. The best-known ascent took place on May 29, 1953, when the New Zealander, Sir Edmund Hillary, and the Sherpa mountaineer, Tenzing Norgay, scaled Everest. To mark their achievement, Hillary buried a small crucifix in the snow. Tenzing added some chocolate, a gift to the Buddhist gods.

Above The south-west face of Mount Everest, the highest mountain in the world.

Left Even with sophisticated equipment, mountaineers still face great danger.

Right An early expedition in the Alps, led by Horace Bénédict de Saussure.

Tourism

Tourism is now a major industry in many mountain regions. Some visitors enjoy hiking or trekking long distances in groups. In Nepal, many Sherpas work as guides and porters. They help trekkers to see some of the great peaks in the Himalayas at close range. One trek leads to Mount Everest in the east. Another takes people on a walk of about 200 miles (320 km) around Mount Annapurna in central Nepal. This trek crosses the Thorung La Pass, which is 17,800 feet (5,425 m) above sea level.

Many people enjoy the thrills of winter sports, of which skiing is the major activity. There are two types of skiing – nordic and alpine. Nordic skiing originated in Scandinavia, where children learn how to ski at an early age. It includes cross-country skiing, a technique practiced on flat or slightly hilly land. Alpine skiing is another name for downhill skiing. Skilled skiers reach speeds of 62 mph (100 kph), and record speeds have exceeded 124 mph (200 kph). Other winter sports in mountain areas include bobsledding, a special form of tobogganing, and ice skating. In the popular ski resorts, winter is the main vacation season, attracting more visitors than in summer.

Hiking, camping, and fishing are popular summer pastimes. In summer, tourists enjoy nature at its most beautiful and peaceful, although some roads may become crowded at the height of the season. Many people enjoy walking vacations in the mountains, exploring the magnificent scenery and discovering the special alpine wildlife.

Large areas of mountains are now preserved in parks, where the animals and plants are left as undisturbed as possible. Yellowstone National Park in Idaho, Montana, and Wyoming, was the world's first national park. Today the United States boasts forty-eight national parks and Canada has another twenty-eight. Many of them preserve block, fold, and volcanic mountains. National parks are now found in most parts of the world.

Skiers in the Rocky Mountains of Utah.

Right The mountain air and superb scenery attract many people to the Swiss Alps.

Below A trekking party in the Himalayan region of Lumding.

Conservation

Despite the setting up of national parks, many mountain areas are threatened by pollution and human mismanagement. Mining is damaging the scenery, while factory wastes and untreated sewage are poisoning some mountain rivers. One of the world's most polluted rivers is the Bogotá River, which flows through the Andes in Colombia. People who drink or even bathe in its waters risk catching many unpleasant diseases. Tourism is another threat, if it is on too large a scale, because it can upset the fragile balance of nature.

However, deforestation (the clearance of forests), overgrazing, and other poor farming methods have done the worst damage. Deforestation and the grazing of goats and sheep have laid bare many mountain regions in Greece, Italy, and southern Spain. The exposed soil has been washed into the sea, and once fertile areas are now barren. Even in remote parts of the Himalayas, extensive deforestation is taking place.

In 1985, the world was alerted to a terrible famine in the mountainous country of Ethiopia. The immediate cause was drought, but deforestation, overgrazing, and overintensive cultivation have stripped the soil of its nutrients, contributing to falling food production. In 1900, forests covered 40 percent of Ethiopia. Today they cover 4 percent.

Soil erosion became a serious problem in the central and eastern United States in the early twentieth century. In 1933, the Tennessee Valley Authority (TVA) was set up to stop the human misuse of the Tennessee River basin, between the Appalachian Mountains and the Mississippi River valley. Forests were planted on bare slopes and dams were built to control flood water. The dams also produced electric power for factories, which provided jobs for farmers whose land had been ruined. Those who stayed on the land were taught better farming methods. Such major projects can repair human damage. But unfortunately, animals and plants made extinct by human exploitation can never be replaced.

Left These Greek mountains were once densely wooded, but grazing and deforestation has left an eroded, barren topsoil.

Much of the wooded slopes of Australian mountains have been devastated by deforestation. However, a number of national parks have now been created to protect these beautiful mountain environments. Pictured at **right** is Mount Bogong in the Bogong National Park, Victoria.

Glossary

Asthenosphere A partly molten layer inside the earth, underlying the solid lithosphere.

Cirque An armchair-shaped hollow in mountain slopes where glacier ice was once formed. Corries and cwms are other names for cirques.

Erosion All the processes, including weathering, running water, moving bodies of ice, and winds, that are involved in wearing away the land.

Fault A fracture (or crack) in the earth's crust, along which the rocks have moved.

Feldspar A group of hard, rock-forming minerals consisting of aluminum silicates of potassium and sodium. Feldspar often makes up granite.

Graben The German name for a rift valley, formed when a block of land sinks between faults.

Ghost town A deserted town, usually in the western United States, once populated during the gold rushes.

Granite A light-colored volcanic rock consisting of quartz and feldspars. Often used in building.

Leeward A word used to describe the side of a slope that is sheltered from the wind.

Lithosphere The solid outer layer of the earth's crust, consisting of rocks and soil.

Magma Molten material inside the earth. When it reaches the surface, it is called lava.

Mica Any of a group of colorless, crystalline minerals formed from cooled magma.

Minerals Elements or compounds (chemical combinations of elements) that make up the earth's crust. Unlike rocks, minerals have a definite chemical composition.

Perennial A plant that continues to grow for several years.

Plate tectonics The theory that explains how plates in the earth's crust form, move, and are destroyed. This theory has helped geologists to understand the reasons for earthquakes, volcanic eruptions, and mountain building.

Pollution The contamination of the air, land, and bodies of water by human activities.

Quartz A colorless crystalline mineral often present in sandstone and granite. Its impure colored varieties include agate and amethyst.

Soil The thin layer of loose material overlying solid rocks. It consists of worn fragments of rock, humus (plant and animal remains), air, water, and various living organisms.

Soil erosion The removal of soil resulting from human misuse of the land. It occurs at a much faster rate than natural erosion.

Temperate zones Those parts of the world situated between the Arctic Circle and the Tropic of Cancer and the Tropic of Capricorn and the Antarctic Circle. A certain type of vegetation flourishes in the particular climate of temperate regions.

Volcano A vent (opening) through which magma, gases, and steam are emitted from the ground. Mountains that form around the vents are also called volcanoes.

Weathering The processes that break up or decay rocks. Mechanical weathering includes the shattering of rocks by frost action. Chemical weathering includes the decay and removal of rock by the action of rainwater.

Windward A word used to describe the side of a slope that is exposed to the wind.

Left The Baltoro glacier in Pakistan, at the foot of K2.

Further reading

Bain, Iain. *Mountains and Earth Movements*. New York: Franklin Watts/Bookwright Press, 1984.
Bain, Iain. *Mountains and People*. Morristown: Silver Burdett, 1982
Brandt, Keith, *Mountains*. Mahwah, NJ: Troll Associates, 1985.
Catchpole, Clive. *Mountains*. New York: Dial Books for Young Readers, 1984.
George, Jean C. *One Day in the Alpine Tundra*. New York: Crowell Junior Books, 1984.

Marcus, Elizabeth. *All about Mountains and Volcanoes*. Mahwah, NJ: Troll Associates, 1984.
Robin, Gordon deQ. *Glaciers and Ice Sheets*. New York: Franklin Watts/Bookwright Press, 1984.
Time-Life Editors, *Volcanoes*. Alexandria: Time-Life Books Inc, 1982.
Uba, Gregory. *Is a Mountain Just a Rock?* Sebastopol, CA: Mina Press, 1984.
Updegraffe, Imelda and Robert. *Mountains and Valleys*. New York: Penguin Books, 1983.

Picture acknowledgments

The publishers would like to thank the following for allowing their photographs to be reproduced in this book: Bruce Coleman Limited 8 (Gerald Cubitt), 12 (Alain Compost), 15 (Dieter & Mary Plage), 21 below (Chris Bonington), 24 below (Leonard Lee Rue III), 26 (Hans Reinhard), 27 (Lynn M Stone), 43 (John R Brownlie), *front cover* inset; Camerapix Hutchison Library 21 above, 30 above, 37 above and below; John Cleare/Mountain Camera 14, 17 below, 23, 24 above (Bill O'Connor), 33 below, 38, 39 above, 40 right, *front cover* main picture; Mary Evans Picture Library 39 below; Geoscience Features Picture Library 6, 18, 19 below, 20, 29 below, 33 above; Jimmy Holmes 29 above, 31; Marion and Tony Morrison South American Pictures 7; Swiss National Tourist Board 11; ZEFA 13 right (W. Stoy), 17 above, 19 above, 28, 35 above and below, 40 left, 41. All illustrations are by Rob Shone.

Index